I Walk by

Faith,

Not by *Sight*

Camille Christian

WESTBOW·
PRESS
A DIVISION OF THOMAS NELSON
& ZONDERVAN

WestBow Press books may be ordered through booksellers or by contacting:

WestBow Press
A Division of Thomas Nelson & Zondervan
1663 Liberty Drive
Bloomington, IN 47403
www.westbowpress.com
1 (866) 928-1240

ISBN: 978-1-4908-6954-4 (sc)
ISBN: 978-1-4908-6955-1 (e)

Library of Congress Control Number: 2015902143

Print information available on the last page.

WestBow Press rev. date: 03/19/2015

Contents

My Personal Testimony

I am a Christian Poet
I write about the
God that I love.
One day I hope to
Meet Him.
The awesome Creator
Above.
'till then I'll share
my story
Of how our relationship
Came to be.
Open your heart
and just listen
To my personal testimony.
I'll take you along an
Intimate journey!

My Faith is based upon the 'Rock'

My faith is based upon the Rock
No one finds it as a shock
I live my life transparently
My faith in Christ is clear
For anyone to see
My faith is based upon the Rock
I worship Him year 'round the clock!

Nature

Near the ocean we sat in peace
Awaiting for the sun to arise
Tides crashed against the shore gently
Undisturbed seemed the world at the time
Ravishing can God's creation be
Even at the most simplest sights.

I worship the Lord Jesus Christ

I worship the Lord Jesus Christ
And trust in Him with all my might
He gives me strength to fight the
Good Fight and the courage
To live my life upright
I worship the lord Jesus Christ
And trust in Him with all my might
His light shines through me very bright!

Play

Placing our hands in the mud
Laughing at our masterpiece
All day we worked hard to create it
Yay! We shouted with glee

The Testimony of a Christian Warrior

There laid the quiet soldier
Facing death so bravely.
For a year or so he fought
In war and served his country
Courageously.
But now his life
Was ending he dreamed
of going home
The thought of dying pained him
And leaving his loved ones alone.
Very faithful of a spouse he was
His family loved him dearly.
He cherished his last moments with
Them and was consoled by the memories.
As he took his last breath he understood
All was not lost after-all
Because Jesus was His Savior
The ultimate victory had been won.
Once he closed his eyes a new
Journey with Christ begun!

The Fight for our Rights ain't Over Yet

The fight for our rights
ain't over just yet
'though 300 years
have passed.
Some may say that
all men are free,
but as for me
I strongly disagree.
Listen carefully to
the echoes of history.
In the news slaves still
cry out and plea.
So I don't know about you
but I know what I believe.
The fight for our rights ain't
over quite yet.
So let's unite and fight
together continuously
for the cause of
'EQUALITY!'

Teach

To teach you must be patient
Every student would like to learn
Assist them in gaining knowledge
Care and they'll appreciate your concern
Hear students out! For once give them a turn.

A Friend of Healing

Kind words are always treasured
A friend of healing knows
Through times of trouble they're with you
Ready to cheer you on

Dream

Dare to live life to its fullest
Reach out to accomplish your goals
Earnestly try your hardest
And eventually your success will unfold
Meditate on the thoughts that uplift your soul

I Love my Community

I love my community
there are plenty of things to do
You can go on nature walks
and learn something new
everyone there is friendly
the festivals are fun to go to
I love the small town of Safety Harbor
and enjoy living there too!

Hope

His hand stretched out toward me
Oppression was removed
Peace overcame my body
Ever since my spirit has been renewed

Winter

When the weather becomes chilly
Inside the house is the place to be
Near the fireplace I feel frizzy
The warm air comforts me
Endlessly I rest there very much at peace
Resisting the cool outdoors so that I don't freeze

How to make the World a Better Place

Work hard to make a better living
Overcome the challenges you face
Reach out to those that need you
Love one another
Don't hate!

Jesus is my Comforter

Jesus is my comforter
He's always there for me.
He takes away my worries
and allows my soul to be free.
If your ever feeling lonely
He'll be there for you too.
All you need to do is ask Him
and He'll comfort you too!

When Jesus died on the Cross

When Jesus died
on the cross
He arose again
He died
for you and I
my friend,
so we may recieve
salvation
and forgiveness
for our sins
That's why
I'll worship Him
until the very end!

Inspire

Influence the world around you
Now is your time to shine
Show off your true potential
Paths of wisdom are divine
Imagine what you could be made of
Relentlessly challenge your mind
Empower those around you and life will be very fine!

Cupid find me a Valentine

Cupid find me a Valentine
I refuse to live my days alone.
With just one shot of your arrow
My lonely days will forever be gone!

Forgive

Fill your mind with happy thoughts
Or be consumed by misery.
Revenge perverses a man's heart
Grace stregthens the inner being.
Influence those around you with love
Vile actions will solve nothing.
Easygoing life can be when you spread peace.

God's Children Faithfully Stand by Him

A peaceful world
Untainted by sin
Is promised to those
That repent.
God's children faithfully
Stand by Him
Awaiting for His will
To be fulfilled.
Long ago he promised
To return again
And take everyone who
Believes in Him.
For certain,
He definitely will.
God never breaks His promises
That's why He's my best friend!

Blessed is the Lord for His Loving Kindness

Thank you lord for
redeeming my soul
and for letting
your blessings unfold!
Life is too precious
To waste in sin
Once you understand
His righteousness.
Blessed is the Lord
Always for His
Loving kindness!

Because Jesus heard my Cries

Because Jesus heard
My cries
His blood was shed
For me.
On the cross He hung
and died.
Now from sin I am
set free.
His life was the
Ultimate sacrifice.
Through Him I have
The victory.
My Savior is the
Risen Christ.
I give Him all
The glory!

What if God was One of Us?

What if God was
one of us?
The question was
Once asked.
The answer was
Revealed the
Day that Jesus
Wept.
He sacrificed His
Life
By taking on
The Father's
Wrath.
'though people
Rejected Him
He stayed on the
Righteous path.
His life was a gift
To us.
Great and Mighty is
the Holy Lamb!
Amen.

God has an Awesome Plan for Us

God has an awesome plan
For us
That's why He redeemed
The world
His will is one that we
Can trust
The Gospel of Christ
Must be heard
Be careful not to fall
Into lust
His plan for us
is superb!

God over the Universe

God over the Universe
All-powerful on top
of Your throne
Your creations are
So diverse.
Allow Your mysteries
To be known.
Humans wander curiously
Down here on Earth.
Miraculous wonders have
You shown!

Jesus Died for Me on Mt. Calvary

Jesus is the promised King
Born through Mary's seed.
His life was sacrifice for me
So I can be freed from sin.
That's why He died on
Mt. Calvary
But He arose again.
Over Death He won
The victory!
Saved are those who
Believe in Him.
A precious gift is God
The Son.
Born one silent night
In Bethlehem!

God's love is for all of Us

Faith becomes perverse
by lust
and can destroy a
person's trust.
Forever God will
Love all of us
But looks at sin
With disgust.
Dwellers in lust can
Not fully be blessed
Because they reveal to
God their distrust.
If in God we claim
To trust
Let's put aside all
Of our lust
And worship Him fully.
Only then, will we
truly be blessed!

Let's have some Fun!

Let's have some
Fun!
All day long we can
Play in the sun.
The school year has
not yet begun.
let's not waste time inside
with boredom.
The summer has brought
Us freedom.
So let's go outside and
Have fun!

I Have a Friend that You can Trust

I have a friend that
You can trust.
He's only seen in the
Best of us.
He'll solve your problems
Without a fuss.
Because of Him my
Life is blessed.
Jesus is my friend that
You can trust!

Free Liberty under the Lord

Free liberty under the law
Of the Lord
Is something that we can
All afford.
Just get into God's
Word
And learn to use it as a
Spiritual sword
Against the Devil of
This world.
Don't allow your mind
To be torn.
Manifest in sin and your life
Will be worn.

Like a Flower my Life has Bloomed

Because the sun shined through
I no longer sing the blues.
My spirit feels renewed
Because the Lord
Removed the gloom
And put me in a
Better mood.
Now I'm singing a
Happier tune!
Like a flower my
Life has bloomed.

There's no doubt Jesus loves You

In your darkest hour
The Lord will take
Care of you.
Pray to Him about
Your issues
And He will see you
Through.
There's no doubt Jesus
Loves you.
You're His number
One pursuit!

Prayer is Good for the Soul

Prayer is good for the soul.
It will never become old.
Pray so your heart won't
Turn cold.
To God let your worries
Be told.
Never be afraid to pray
Of something bold.
Life with Him is richer
Than gold!
So continuously pray and
Witness His blessings unfold.

Through thick and thin

Through thick and thin
God will be your best friend
His love lasts forever
From beginning to the end!

Jesus set the Perfect Example for Us

Jesus set the perfect example
for us
In Him we should put all of
Our trust
Follow His example and you'll
Truly be blessed!

Through Him Redemption was Sworn

The nation of Israel was
Forewarned
That our Savior Jesus would
Be born.
And suffer a life of humiliation
and scorn,
but from His longsuffering
redemption was sworn.

My Savior bore the Cross for Me

My Savior bore the cross
For me,
Because of Him my life's
Set free.
He paid the price on
Mt. Calvary.
That proves how Awesome a
God He can be!

The Word of God is Divine

The word of God
Is divine
To guide those who are
Spiritually blind.
The resurrection of Christ
Is a sign
God will accept people
Of all kinds!

The Lord gave me Peace of Mind

The Lord gave me peace
Of mind
When I was spiritually
Blind
He comforts me all the
Time
His nature is so gentle
And kind
Because of Him my
Light shines!

Set your Life's Foundation on Him

Set your Life's foundation
on Him
And a new journey in life
Will begin
Don't let your life be destroyed
By sin
Or allow your enemies
to win
Adapt Jesus Christ as your
Friend
And conquer your life battles
Through Him

A Beautiful Night

Laying on top of my roof a
Beautiful night
A million stars stretched
Across the sky
I admired the heavens in
The moonlight
Like a giant pearl it stood
Clear in sight

Don't believe the Devil's Lies

Don't believe the Devil's
Lies
The Lord will deliver you
From your strife
He hears all of your cries
At night
And has a great plan to
Transform your life!

A World Paralyzed by Sin

We live in a world paralyzed
By sin
Oblivious to those who
Shallowly fit in
Be careful when you choose as
Your friends
And whose hands your life
Depends
When you examine their hearts
Is Christ within?
Do they stick with you through
Thick and thin?
If not, they're truly your enemy
Not your friend
And it's wiser to put those
Relationships to an end.

Words can be a Blessing or a Curse

With words God created
the Universe
and separated the heavens
from the Earth.
Words can be a blessing
Or a curse.
Despite being abstract words
can hurt,
If used in a way that's
perverse.

I Walk by Faith not by Sight

Once upon a peaceful
Night
I stayed up with a disturbed
mind
staring up into the deep
Blue sky
Dreaming of a better
Life
And then I began to
Frantically cry
You see today I planned
To end my life
Although I was a soon to
Be bride
I knew I should be happy
But instead I felt hurt
inside
My fiance was wicked and
Very impolite
He beat me half to death one
Time
I felt discouraged and tuned
in the Devil's lies
I was convinced to escape
him I must commit
suicide

So that night for certain I would
Die
But then I heard a soft whisper
that came from inside
It made me put the pills
aside
For sure it was my friend
Jesus Christ
He healed me and stopped me
from ending my life
and reminded me that true love was
gentle and kind
Immediately I felt deep healing take
place from inside
I went back to sleep with peace
Of mind
In my darkest hour he saved my
Life!
Now I walk by faith and not by Sight

The Lord will see you Through

Success is a mountain that you
Must climb
Don't be ashamed to use your
Mind
You'll accomplish your goals
Overtime
The Lord will see you through
By and by!

Jesus was born to be King

Jesus was born to be
King
And rules over every-
thing
I give Him glory when
I sing
He's worthy of honor
And praise
On heaven and Earth forever
He will reign!

He'll open Heaven's Gate

God makes no mistakes
Jesus was sent to die for our
Own sake
From Death He's the only
Escape
But we decide our own
Fate
Accepting Him is a decision we
must all make
As long as you're living it's not
Too late
Trust in Him and He'll open
heaven's gate

Jesus sends signs

Jesus sends signs
To those that are
Spiritually blind
His word is so divine
And truthful all the time

Thank You Lord for everything You do!

Thank You Lord for everything
You do!
And for the trails and tribulation
You
Have helped me pull
Through
Great barriers in my life You
have removed
that's why I have surrendered my
entire life to you

The word of God is no Fallacy

The word of God is no
Fallacy
If you trust in Him you'll
See
Sin weakens human beings
Definitely
And ruins the faith of those
That believe

Jesus is my Lifeboat

Jesus is my lifeboat
He's with me everywhere
I go
He sends down His heavenly
Hosts
And guides me by the Holy
Ghost!

He's Watching over You

There's nothing you
Can do
To stop the lord from
Loving you
He's watching over
You
And knows everything
You do

The Season of Spring

Sunflowers sprang from underneath the dirt
Pastures once plain are now full with color
Rainy days nourish the plants and trees of the Earth
I patiently wait for the weather to change it's course
Nature is maturing during this season of rebirth
Glorious are all the creations that God supports

'Cause the Lord set me Free

Because the Lord set me
Free
I no longer feel
Guilty
Neither am I in
Misery
I'm as happy as I can
Be
Because the Lord set me
Free!

The Lord paid our Way

Since the Lord paid
Our way
Let's be the best we
can today
It's immature to
Say
That we're not perfect
Anyway
Although we make
Mistakes
If we try we'll be
Okay
After all since God paid
Our way
We're going to make it
anyway
So let's make a better
Living day by day

God Will Take You In

Open up your hearts within
And God will take you in
Don't allow your hearts
Be hardened by sin
Humble yourselves and
Learn to forgive

'Evermore shall Love Endure

Help those who are in need
Operate under the Lord
Plant the most fruitful seeds
'Evermore shall love endure

Good Friday

On Good Friday we celebrate
Jesus's birth
His crucifixion and
Resurrection from
The Earth
We await patiently
For His return
As a bride waiting for
Her groom

Lord I Admire You

Lord I admire you
And everything you
Do
You're an awesome
God too!
That's why I worship
you

A Love Poem

I enjoy being
with you
and everything
we do.
You're really
Cute!
You're coolest
one in school
Very smart
and funny too.
After all that we've
Gone through
I desire to be with you!

Oh, My Lord Up Above

Oh, my Lord up
Above
You're the one I'm
Dreaming of
Because you show me
Lots of love
I worship you!

When the Storm came Through

When the storm came
Through
The Lord was watching
Over you
Your calamities he
Knew
'though you never had
A clue
He helped you survive
Them too
A stronger person you've
Grown into
All because His awesome
Plan for you

Christ Preached Love not Hate

Christ preached love
Not hate
So let's not discriminate
In life let's show a little
More grace
And learn how to
Appreciate
Let's put aside our
Differences
to become teammates
And work together
to
Make this world a
Better place

The Day Jesus died on Pentecost

The day Jesus died on
Pentecost
He saved the lives of those
Who were lost
An innocent man He died
On the cross
But to save sinners His life
Was worth the cost

As a Child of God you are Blessed

As a child of God you
Are blessed
You hold the keys to
Success
All you need is to try
Your best
There's no excuse for
Anything less

What Wonderful Man is He

Jesus lived very
humbly
And served those who
Were in need
He healed the oppressed
And set them free
And died on the cross to
Save you and me
He spent His life doing
Great deeds
And was all about making
Peace
What a wonderful man
Is He!

God's children make a Joyful Sound

God's children make a
Joyful sound
Because the time is
Coming 'round
For their Savior to come
Back down
'though His feet won't
Touch the ground
They'll meet Him in the
Heavenly clouds
The Lord will heal them from
Their wounds
And by His side righteously they
Will stand proud

Before Jesus Changed my Game

Before Jesus changed my
Game
I used to live my life in
For fame
In being sinful I felt no
Shame
Until the Devil began to cause
Me pain
His deceitfulness drove me
Insane
Now I prefer not to live the
same
Instead I'm living toward a
higher aim
My life is no longer
Lame
And Jesus is the one to
Blame
For the better person that
I became

His name is Jesus Christ

(A short hymnal)

(Sing!) He is the Redeemer of
believers
The Savior of all
lives
The Healer of the
broken
His name is Jesus
Christ
He'll never forsake or
leave you
He'll guide you when
your blind
Just trust in Him through
hardships
His love lasts a
lifetime!

I can't live without
You
You're everywhere I
Go
The Holy Spirit inside
Me
Is there to let me
Know

There's no need to
Worry
'Cause you'll take
care of me
As long as I just
listen
My life is stress
Free!
Cause you're the…

Redeemer of
believers!
The Savior of all
lives
The Healer of the
broken
Your name is Jesus
Christ
You'll never forsake or
leave me
You'll guide me when
I'm blind
I'll trust in You through
hardships
Your love lasts a
lifetime!

Thank you Lord for
hearing my
cries
And for giving me peace
of mind
You are the strength
of my life
Awesome source of
Eternal life

The Lord's Love is Precious to Me

The Lord's love is precious
To me
More than any carnal possessions
Can be
'though His love is priceless it'll
Last forever
While expensive materials will rot
That you gather,
The Lord's love is precious
To me
Greater than any worldly treasures
Can be!

Lay your Worries at the Cross

(A short hymnal)

(Sing!) Jesus' message to the
lost
Is to lay your worries at
the cross
No matter what the problem
May be
He paid the price for all
our deeds!

There's no sin too high
a fee
His blood couldn't cover
on Mt. Calvary!
Someday our Lord will
Return again
So receive the message
And cherish it!

No longer will people be
Filled with doubt
When they see Him standin'
Up in the clouds
The righteous, wicked, rich
and poor
Will all bow humbly before
the Lord!

Jesus' message to the
lost
Is to lay your worries at
the cross
No matter what the problem
May be
He paid the price for all
our deeds!

God's everlasting Love

God's everlasting love will never
Leave you
Despite how much trouble you
Get into
God's knows and sees everything that
You do
'though you sin behind
doors
He's watching over
 you
God's everlasting love will never
Leave you!

Help me not to be a Slave to Sin

(A short hymnal)

(Sing!)

Help me not to be a
Slave to sin
And drink wine of
the Prostitute,
For just a moment
I desire to fit in
And gain some
Worldly comforts
Too,
Give me strength until
The very end
To overcome harassment
and Abuse,
'Though I was ostracized
And I was victimized
My rebellion still has
No excuse.
Help me manifest in holy
Righteousness
So that I'm as good of
Person as you!
Help me not to be a
slave to sin
So that I can be a faithful
Servant unto you!

Be the Salt in all the Earth

(Sing!)

(A short hymnal)
To God's children in the
World
Be the salt in all the
Earth!
Live in harmony with the
Word
Until the day of His
return!

You're the ones our Savior
picked
To be the vessels of His
Ship!

So work together in one
accord
Be the salt in all the
Earth!
Tune in with His Holy
word
'Till the day the of His
return!

May God's Grace be with You

May God's grace be with
You
Everywhere you
Go
May His light shine
Upon you
And encourage you to
carry on
Through trials and
Tribulations
You'll stand triumphantly
All 'cause His grace shines
Upon you
You've won the
Victory!

We will bring Glory to the King

(A short hymnal)

(Sing!)   O what joy does it

bring

To hear all God's children

Sing

That through Christ

Salvation was

Won

Blessed is the Father,

Holy Spirit

And Son!

Because He gave his life

For us

In His eternal will we'll

Trust

We'll go to church to worship

And praise

And the Holy Spirit will

Work through us!

We will bring glory to the
King
Whenever we praise Him and
we sing!
Forever we will give a joyous shout
And honour
His name without a
doubt!

When the journey of this life
Feels long,
And we lack the strength to
Carry on,
We'll just remember to
keep prayin'
on
And our faith in Christ
Will keep
Us standin' strong!

(lead singer)   Bring glory to the Prince
of Peace
Every night before you go to
Sleep
Sing praises to the Prince of
Peace
His love is great for you and
Me!

(chorus)　　　　We will bring glory to the
King
Whenever we praise Him and
we sing!
Forever we will give a joyous shout
And honour
His name without a
doubt!

Walk in the Spirit

(A short hymnal)

(Sing!)

Walk in the Spirit
Walk in the light
Christ is the source
of eternal life!
Walk in the Spirit
Walk by His side
Allow your persona
To shine really bright!
Walk in the Spirit
Live life upright
The word of God is
the bread of life!
Walk in the Spirit
Walk in the light
And receive His
blessings
With delight!

Sow Seeds of Righteousness

Sow seeds of righteousness
And
Spread the Gospel of
Truth!
Spread hope indiscriminately
So
The world hears the Message
 too!
Manifest in righteousness
so
Others receive the Good
News!
Work hard 'till harvest
Day
For the Lord will be returnin'
Soon!
Stand strong in your discipleship
And
Witness your seeds of faith
Bloom!

Give me the Faith of a Musterseed

Give me the faith of a
 musterseed
So I can move mountains
like you.
Give me the faith of a
musterseed
So that I can be stronger
like you.
Give me the faith of a
musterseed
I desire to understand
the truth.

The Chains of Oppression was Broken

The Chains of oppression was
Broken
That the Devil had over
Me
The Chains of Oppression was
Broken
The day the Lord received
Me
When the bondage of Satan
Was strong
And to life I barely hung
On
The chains of oppression was
Broken
Because the Lord delivered
Me!

Printed in the United States
By Bookmasters